The Meaning of Life Coffee Shop

A Book About Finding Your Way

Matt Tracy

Chiloé Press

Published in the United States

by Chiloé Press

THE MEANING OF LIFE COFFEE SHOP

Printed in the United States of America.

www.matttracyauthor.com

Library of Congress Cataloging-in-Publication Data

Name: Tracy, Matt, author

Title: The Meaning of Life Coffee Shop: A Book About Finding Your Way / Matt Tracy

Description: First Edition. | California: Chiloé Press, [2022]

ISBN 978-1-7366459-4-9 (paperback)

ISBN 978-1-7366459-5-6 (ebook)

Classification LCSH: BF637.P3 Applied Psychology/Peace of Mind

First Edition: February 2022

10 9 8 7 6 5 4 3 2 1

ACCLAIM FOR HAPPY HERE AND NOW

Also By Matt Tracy

If you want to be happier, you've got to read *Happy Here and Now*! Although I wrote my own book on happiness, I was still blown away by Matt's profound insights, fascinating stories, and the powerful exercises he provides that made an immediate difference in my life. Each time I pick it up, I love it even more. Highly recommended!

—Carol Kline, #1 *New York Times* bestselling co-author of *Happy for No Reason, Love for No Reason*, five books in the *Chicken Soup for the Soul* series and *Conscious Luck: Eight Secrets to Intentionally Change your Fortune*

Loved it! This book nails it. It looks from lots of angles at what causes happiness and tells you what to do to get there.

Dr Fred Luskin, Author of *Forgive for Good: A Proven Prescription for Health and Happiness*

To Maria
Who knows
True love isn't gazing adoringly
into each other's eyes
It's looking ahead with curiosity, side by side

1

I FOUND IT WHEN I was searching for something else.

That's how it often goes. Your keys are not in your pants, and not on the table by the door, so you root through the gym bag and the jeans you were wearing the day before and then out of desperation you look in your underwear drawer. Nestled in back is the passport you couldn't find last week and finding that was more important than the keys that got you started looking in the first place.

That day, I was sitting at my desk, fantasizing about how I would quit my job. In my daydream, I walked into my boss's office and told him I had gotten an offer from another company. I imagined the speech I would make and his surprise. I imagined him making me an offer of a promotion and a raise if I would stay. I paused on an image of me shaking my head as I calmly refused. I must have had a dreamy expression on my face when my he strode into my office in person, closing the door behind him.

"We have to talk." He said as he sat in the chair across from me. "The auditors found your little bank account."

I shook my head. "Which one is that?"

"The one where the customer discount funds were going. We know everything."

I shrugged my shoulders and frowned. "I'm still confused. Maybe you should start at the beginning."

He leaned forward, putting his forearms on my desk. "You know what I'm talking about. It doesn't make sense to deny it. Your fingerprints are all over the code. The only question now is whether the authorities are going to get involved."

I held my hands out in front of me. "I'm really lost. I know you think I should know this but explain it to me. Please."

"I can't." He pushed off my desk as he stood up. "We need to have witnesses to any further conversations. All I'm saying is you're in deep trouble. Nobody else knows anything yet. Take the day off, and we'll decide what to do with you tomorrow."

So I went for a walk, confused, downhill toward home. I had no idea what he was talking about, but I had been sent home like I had done something, and I was possibly in trouble with the law for it. My head was buzzing from the anxiety like electricity was flowing from it. I had a vision of one of those lightning generator balls that they had in science exhibitions when I was a kid where everyone holds hands in a circle and when the last person touches the ball, everyone's hair starts to stand on end.

I was sure my hair was standing on end right then. The worst part was not knowing why.

I might be fired. That got me thinking about the first job I had been fired from. It was at the Super Seven gas station. It was the cheapest gas in town, so it was a busy station. My friend and I worked there together three nights a week in high school. He got the job first, then recommended me. A lot of the customers paid in cash. Sometimes there were five or six cars filling up. We didn't sit in a booth and push buttons either. We were out among the cars, resetting the pumps, taking money, making change, and helping people if they needed it. The shifts flew by.

Every half hour or so we would empty all the big bills out of the cash register and put them through a slot in the floor into the safe that couldn't be opened until morning. I didn't work there long, because one day, the till came up short and we were out of work. I never did figure out what happened. I knew I hadn't taken anything I shouldn't have, and I was pretty sure my friend didn't either, but we had been running and making change all night so anything could have happened. This situation felt eerily similar.

I felt like I might be in trouble for something I didn't do, and never be able to find out the truth.

Without warning, I had a free day, but it wasn't one I could enjoy. I was too anxious. It was like a dream where I couldn't find the class I was supposed to have been in all semester. I felt like I should have known what my boss was talking about, but I just didn't. So, I wandered. The day was sunny and warm, with a cool breeze blowing off the ocean. Looking down the glass and asphalt canyons between the buildings, I could see glimpses of sailboats on the bay. In spite of what I had done that I couldn't remember doing and was probably going to get fired for or maybe go to jail, my spirits lifted as I walked and breathed.

San Francisco gives these days to its residents to help us through the grey days of summer. After a week of fog, the sun breaks through and reminds us how beautiful the city can be as the morning light makes gold streaks on the buildings. The week before, under grey skies, it had been easy to forget that the rest of the country was struggling with triple digit heat and humidity and the fog protected us from all that like a leafy tree on a summer day. Then a day like this happens and we can forgive all the fog.

As I turned down a street, I remembered that there was a Philz coffee shop in this neighborhood. I could go there. Coffee always makes me feel better. I made a right turn at the next corner. A truck blocked the sidewalk, so I turned onto a side street, keeping the location of the Philz in my mind. If I turned left then right then left again, I would still be on track.

I turned into an alley off the side street, walking past delivery trucks and garbage dumpsters. A half a block up the alley a crew was moving a large wooden crate out of a window two stories up, and caution tape kept me from going any further. So, I turned left again into a smaller alley. I started to worry about where this was taking me, but I'm a big guy. I scare people, not the other way around. I pushed on.

Just a bit ahead the alley opened into a larger street. I could see the cars at the end of it and people walking by. But on my left was a small storefront, just a doorway with a window beside it, and on the window was a mole drawn in a few strong black lines, like a Japanese brush painting. Under the mole were the words *Coffee Shop and Bookstore*. I made a seemingly trivial decision that changed my life. I opened the door and stepped inside, and I found something I didn't know I was looking for.

2

A BELL ON THE door tinkled as I entered, and I breathed deeply the smell of coffee brewing. At the back of the small square room a man sat on a stool behind a wooden counter, reading a book. He looked up and smiled as I entered. I could see a coffee grinder behind him, and multicolored ceramic cups on shelves above that. Near the window were two chairs and a round granite topped table just big enough for two cups of coffee.

Varnished wooden bookshelves filled with books lined one side of a hallway leading toward the back. The hallway was well-lit with warm tones, as if a small part of a library had been dropped there.

On the wall to the right, between the front window and the counter, three questions were hand-painted with the same strong brush strokes beneath another mole. The questions were at eye level and took up the whole wall.

Am I moving toward who I'm meant to be?
If I died today, what would I regret?
Am I being kind?

I read the questions slowly, thinking about what they meant to me. I must have stood there for a minute, staring at the writing on the wall, pondering.

Am I moving toward who I'm meant to be?

As I stood there I thought, "I don't know who I'm meant to be." That was one of my problems. It felt like I was stumbling through a dark room, hearing other people finding things and exclaiming about them and I was walking around with my hands out in front of me hoping not to bang my shins on a table or run into a door. Occasionally, I would find something interesting, but I didn't know how I stumbled on it or how to find another thing like it.

One of my friends has known since he was in fourth grade that he wanted to be a doctor. It must have been comforting to always have a direction in life. Me, I wandered one way and the other, not knowing where to go. Sometimes, I had listened to the advice of someone else, and went where they thought I should go. That hadn't worked so well. I didn't think I was moving toward who I was meant to be, at least not very quickly. And if I was, how would I know?

I shook my head to clear the thoughts and looked over at the guy behind the counter. After a second, he raised his head and smiled at me again. He wasn't old, but he wasn't young, and he didn't fit the profile of your usual barista. His hair was neatly cut, dark with just a hint of grey, and he was clean-shaven. He had on a pair of jeans and a button-up shirt, and he could have been one of my bosses, a tech executive. Except that somehow, he couldn't have been. I tried to figure out the difference. Well, his face, for one. His face looked relaxed, like he had just come back from a Hawaiian vacation, and he still had the leftover inner glow from a week of listening to the wind in the trees and watching the horizon for whales. He looked at me with a pleasantly expectant expression on his face. A hint of humor gleamed in his eyes, like he was thinking of a joke he wanted to tell me. "Good morning. I don't think we've met. I'm Ivan."

"Hi, I'm Scott. I got kind of lost in the questions on the wall."

"That's not unusual for new visitors. I should say, it's not unusual for new visitors who end up coming back a lot. Some people never notice them."

"I was looking for the Philz and saw your sign. You have coffee?"

"Yes. It's French press, not pour over," he said, picking up a stainless-steel pitcher with a knob on top. "It's good though."

"I like the drawing on the front window. What's the name of this place?"

"It's called the MOL."

"It was either that or Gopher. You know, like, 'Who wants to Gopher Coffee?'"

"That would have been a good name." He raised his chin a little toward me and asked, "You have time to drink it here?"

It was a question, but it sounded like a statement. I felt like the storm troopers must have felt when Obi Wan Kenobi says, "These aren't the droids you're looking for." I might have thought I didn't have time to drink it here when I came in, but as soon as he said it, I was sure I had the time.

"Yes, I do have a few minutes to drink it here." I looked down the hallway. "Is that the bookstore down there?"

"We don't have much space, so we don't have many books, but I recommend any of them."

"You're the owner?"

"He put the top on the French press. "Yes, one of them. My wife and I own this shop."

"Why did you call it Mole?"

"For Meaning Of Life. MOL. The E on the end is implied, and we get to have a cute logo. Why don't you browse the bookshelves and head out back? I'll bring you the coffee when it's ready to drink."

Meaning of life? Of course, I had been looking for that too. Isn't everyone? I might have been looking a little more frantically at that time than other people, but I think that's a human condition. We want to know why we're here, and what will make us feel like our time here mattered.

Even before the strangeness with my boss earlier that day, I had been fighting a sense of futility all year. I was working for a company that was making specialized software to help other companies manage their in-house workload. Ours was best for businesses selling to other businesses, not to consumers. It was interesting work, but it was helping companies to be better at being efficient companies while they sold things to other companies. It seemed circular, kind of like a snake eating its own tail. For me, there wasn't much heart there. I kept feeling like something was missing, but I couldn't put words to it.

My friend who always knew he wanted to be a doctor had another advantage over me. He knew that what he was doing mattered. Despite all the changes in the business of doctoring, it's a part of the job description: Make people's lives better through medicine. But how does anyone else make sure they're not wasting their talents on things that don't matter?

In addition, I was putting in long hours trying to get ahead. It seemed to be what everyone did at the company. I worked, ate, slept, and drank. Alcohol and coffee. More coffee than alcohol, luckily, but alcohol was gaining ground. I was feeling worn down and sluggish. Every day felt the same, flat and gray, like a June day in San Francisco where the fog settles in high in the sky and it stays that way all day, with no wind to blow it in or out. No clouds to create any interest. No sun peeking through with a hint of blue skies in the afternoon. I knew I didn't want to keep doing what I was doing, but I didn't know where to start looking for something else. I figured that if they fired me, I would be forced to decide, but what would it be?

Here's how bad it had gotten. One day, sitting in my office, I felt the building move as if a truck had run into it. That's how an earthquake starts. Everything moves a little, and your brain searches for an answer, because buildings don't move like that. So, your brain decides that a big truck must have hit the building. When you've lived in California long enough, you start to think you can tell the difference between the small ones that happen a couple of times a year, and the ones you have to worry about. One way the big ones differ from the small ones is that the big ones often start with a jolt, trucklike, rest for a second or two, then the big shaking starts. This earthquake was like that. It jolted, rested, then started again. When it started again, the adrenaline kicked in, and I started to look around to make sure there was nothing that would fall on my head. Then I looked under my desk to see if I could crawl under there with the space heater and the garbage can.

The other thing I noticed was a sense of anticipation. For a moment, I was hoping for an earthquake because then something meaningful would happen. There would be action and people to help and things to fix. It was a fleeting feeling, but it was there. The earthquake was fleeting too. It wasn't a big one, just a pretender, and the day quickly went back to normal. I couldn't help thinking that the feeling of anticipation was a bad sign for how my life was, and that morning things had gotten worse.

Leaving Ivan in the front of the store, I wandered down the hall looking at the books. A lot of them I recognized. I hadn't read very many though. I chose one called *Almost Everything*.

At the end of the hallway, light came through a frosted glass window in a door. To the right was another door that opened into what looked like a cozy well-lit living room with couches and small tables snugly nestled together. There was art on the walls, and the room looked inviting, but I didn't go in. I just peeked through the doorway then opened the other door and stepped out into a small square patio.

I say patio, but it felt like an oasis. Morning sun bounced off one of the walls of the building next door, lighting up the space. A fountain in the corner looked like a jagged piece of granite weighing a couple hundred pounds had been stood on end and a hole drilled through the length of it. Water burbled out the hole in the top making a pleasing sound as it hit the smaller rocks at the bottom. Little yellow finches flew down, dunked themselves in the water at the top of the rock, and flew away. Then hummingbirds came and buzzed stationary in the air a foot from the fountain for a couple seconds before settling in for a dunk themselves. Plants were growing along the edges of the patio, and a wisteria vine flowered on a trellis. Two cast iron tables with padded wooden chairs invited coffee drinkers, and a couple of outdoor easy chairs made of what looked like plastic wicker with soft looking cushions beckoned to readers. There was nobody in the patio, but it felt like the patio had been waiting for me to show up.

I sat at one of the tables with the book that I had picked up from inside and started to read.

Ivan came out with the coffee and asked if he could sit down at the table with me. I nodded toward the other chair and smiled.

As he sat down, he said, "I see you found *Almost Everything*. What attracted you to that one in particular?"

"I think it was the title."

"Yeah, that title draws you in. I think my favorite part is when she says, *Truth comes in small moments and visions, not galaxies and canyons,* but you'll have your own favorite part.

I took a trial sip of my coffee. The cup had a generous handle that felt good in my hand. "I think I already do. When I sat down just now, I opened it at random and read the passage that says, *Peace of mind is an inside job, unrelated to fame, fortune, or whether your partner loves you.* It felt like it was written for my situation right now. I could use some peace of mind."

"That happens in books. If I ask myself a question the answer often turns up in what I'm reading. It's not just books. People bring answers too, but you have to be careful because people often tell you what's right for them, and you might get confused and think it's right for you. The people who come here have read a lot of books and asked a lot of questions. If you ask them a question, they'll tell you how they've found the answer to that question, then encourage you to look for the answer in a place you might not have thought of looking."

He had a stillness about him. He didn't fidget or scratch or look around like most people do when they talk. I stopped myself from stirring the coffee just to try to not move at all for a moment. I stared, motionless, at the coffee cup for a couple seconds then looked up. "So, if I ask a question and open a book, I might find an answer, but if I ask a question of someone here on this patio, I'll probably get an answer quicker?"

"It is called the Meaning of Life Coffee Shop. We tend to get a certain type of customer. Want to hear about a time when a book answered a question so directly that I couldn't call it coincidence?"

He turned his head as the bell on the front door rang.

"I'll be back in a bit. Enjoy your coffee and reading."

I turned back to the book but couldn't make myself read it. Too many thoughts crowded my mind.

A couple of weeks earlier, my friend Jason had told me that his company was looking for someone like me and had said he could get me an interview. His company always seemed more exciting than mine, but it also seemed like a more high stress environment.

I hang around Jason when I want a burst of frenetic energy mixed with angst and confusion. When I was a kid, a friend of mine made the mistake of eating a hotdog and a soda at a carnival and then going on the tilt-a-whirl. We were beside each other, standing up in our cages, our heads sucked back into the padding by centripetal force, looking at the ground one moment and the sky the next when I heard him say, "I think I'm going to heave."

I looked over at him out of the corner of my eye and was glad I was upwind of him. At the same time, I tried to see who was on the other side, about to be surprised by a face full of recycled carnival food. He got off the ride without anything coming up, but the image of him running down the metal stairs, stumbling around in circles on the straw covered ground, and throwing up in front of the balloon-dart booth is burned in my mind. Now replace soda with Red Bull and vodka, and you have a day with Jason.

I went for the interview. Jason's company felt like a good fit for Jason, with a sharp-edged energy pervading the place. The company was moving fast, and everyone there was in a hurry to get where they were going. Logically, I was pretty sure I could do the job, but in my stomach, I felt like I did on my first day of middle school. Everyone seemed bigger than me, and knew where everything was, and I couldn't remember my locker combination and had lost my list of classes. I felt a sense of excitement mixed with dread when I thought about working there.

I got a job offer from Jason's company. And I was considering it. I would have had to move to LA, but that would have been a plus because my girlfriend, Isabella, had moved there for a better job, asking me to come when I could.

Isabella. That's another subject. Let me talk about fear and adrenaline and pain in my stomach and anticipation first.

I was considering the new job because I wasn't sure whether the feeling of dread and excitement and confusion was good or bad. Any time I start something new and important, I'm not sure about my abilities. I spend way too much time worrying if I'm good enough to do the thing I signed up for. I know this is normal for me, and part of anything worthwhile is that I'll have to work through the feelings of insufficiency and self-doubt. Usually, I do that by putting my head down and pushing through them like they were branches hanging over a path. They'll scratch as I go by, but in a while, I'll be past them and on to a clearer walkway. What I didn't know was whether the gnawing in my stomach was normal fear that I should push through or whether it was something else that I should listen to. How could I tell the difference between the two?

When he came back, Ivan asked, "You ready to hear about a book answering a question?"

I sat up straighter in my chair, gestured toward his chair, and said, "Sure."

He sat down across from me at the table, crossed his legs at the knee, and leaned back a little. "I was driving along the freeway one afternoon in winter. It was cold and kind of hazy. I looked over toward the hills to the west and saw two suns. Side by side. I looked back at the road, then at the suns again. They were still there. At first, I thought the moon must be next to the sun, but then I realized it couldn't be full and be beside the sun. I had no idea what it could be. I thought it must be some type of refraction phenomenon but had no way of figuring it out. This was the days before you could just Google 'two suns in the sky' and get the answer.

"That evening at supper, I told my wife about it, and we couldn't figure out what it could have been. Later that night, I climbed into bed beside her and opened the book I had just started reading. On the first page that I read, the main character walks out early in the morning to feed the chickens and sees two suns in the sky. He says to himself, 'Here I am 65 years old, and I'm seeing my first sundog.

"In the same day, I saw a sundog and didn't know what it was, wondered out loud what it was, and the first page of the first book I opened told me the answer. What are the odds of that? It made me start looking for that to happen again with less obvious questions. I started to ask a question and wait patiently for an answer to show up. Books are one of the ways the answers have come to me. People are another. Unexpected detours are another." He pointed toward my almost empty cup. "Would you like more coffee?"

"I think I need to keep walking. It seems to help with my confusion. I'll be back."

"Yes, please, come back. I think you're someone who could be a regular here. Would you like to take that book?"

"Yes. Do you mean buy it, or borrow it?"

"That depends. If you're going to read it and return it, then borrow it. If you want to keep it or write in it, maybe you should buy it. You don't have to decide right now."

"Before I go, I have to ask one more thing. The questions on the wall: are they about the meaning of life?"

"Yes." He smiled like he was pleased I had asked. "By asking yourself those questions as you go through your life, you'll find the meaning of life that fits you. That's important. It isn't anyone else's meaning of life because that wouldn't work for you. It's the meaning of your life, how you imagine it and how you live it."

3

AS I WALKED, I tried to figure out what my boss had meant about a bank account and code with my fingerprints on it and kept running into a dead end.

The second job I got fired from, I knew exactly why. I was working in a donut shop from 5 pm to closing. That's a great job for a teenage boy. At the end of the night, any donuts left from the day had to be thrown away. Or eaten. Or I could take them home and give them to my friends. I could eat as many donuts as I wanted. You would think that I wouldn't like donuts after having so many, but I still do, today, especially the old-fashioned ones with the crevasses on top.

It wasn't very busy in the donut shop at night and my job was to make the cake donuts for the next day. I mixed the dough in a huge industrial mixer, emptied it into the donut dough dispenser, got the oil to the right temperature, and started turning the crank to drop the donuts, perfectly formed, one donut per turn of the crank, from the dispenser into the oil. By the time the oil was full of sizzling donuts, it was time to start from the first ones dropped, flipping them with a couple oversized chopsticks. When they were all flipped, I started at the beginning again, taking them out, crispy and hot, and putting them on racks. They would be iced the next morning. Then I cleaned the machines, wiped down the racks and the counters, mopped the floors and got it ready for the next morning. In between, I sold donuts to customers.

The donut shop was on the far side of town by a rival high school. Not long after I started working there, a couple girls from that high school started hanging out with me there. After I had finished making donuts for the next day, I had a lot of freedom to sit in a booth with them talking and drinking sodas before I had to start cleaning.

One night, one of the girls came in by herself. She pulled a joint out of her pocket, waved it in front of my face and asked if I wanted to smoke a little and make out in the back room. Just a little later, when the owner unlocked the back door and walked in, she had her shirt part way off, there was a half-smoked joint on the counter, and I was definitely not minding the cash register. I got home early that night.

That was the last job I had been fired from. This one might be another, but there was nothing I could do but walk with my thoughts.

So, I kept going back to the coffee shop in my mind, especially the patio. You know how when you've just met someone, and you know there's something special there? Maybe you had a date, maybe two, but you keep daydreaming a little as you remember the way they crinkle their eyes when they smile, or something they said. It was like that. I kept thinking about sitting at one of those tables on the patio with the edge of the cast iron vines from the table making a mark on my wrist as my hand rested on a mug of coffee, having a conversation about something important. Maybe about the meaning of life.

4

I DIDN'T READ THE book at home. I thought about the new job and LA and called Isabella. Three months before, when she took her new job, she hadn't really asked me what I thought of her moving. She just told me she was going and that she loved me, but she had to follow her career. So, we didn't break up, but she moved away without really thinking about what I wanted, which I guess I played a part in because I didn't really know what I wanted either. With me acting like I was lost, it probably felt natural for her to take the lead.

Laying on the couch, feet up on the arm, I pushed her photo on my phone. Almost as soon as she picked up she asked, "When are you moving down here? I miss you."

"I don't know. That offer from Jason's company makes it easy, doesn't it? I mean, there's nothing holding me here now. You're there, I have a job there."

Her voice got more sultry. "I'm here, wearing almost nothing, waiting for you to come to me."

"Don't move. I'm getting in the car now. If I drive fast, I can be there in five hours."

She laughed. "I wonder if I can hold this sexy pose that long without getting a cramp."

I sat up, and reached for my water. "Hey, something strange happened at work today. My boss came into my office and accused me of diverting funds from the company into my personal bank account, then told me to take the rest of the day off while they decided what to do. He wouldn't give me any details"

"What? Did you do that?"

I was surprised that she would ask. She knows me. I think I let a bit of petulance seep into my voice as I answered. "No. I have no idea what he's talking about, and I worry that if they start accusing me of something, I'll be trying to prove I didn't do something that I had no knowledge of. Like in the dark ages. Prove to me that you're not a witch. How?"

"Well, if they fire you, at least you have another job to go to," she said, in an airy tone.

"I'm not really sure I want that job. It comes with so much more stress than the one I have."

Her voice softened a little as she murmured, "It doesn't have to be that job. It just has to be one near me. I miss you. I'm not having an easy time getting started here. My team keeps doing things without telling me. It's almost like they don't want me here. I know it'll get better, but it would be easier if you were here with me."

"If we had made the decision together to move, we might be there together."

In my mind I could see her gather her strength as she replied, "Don't go there. You know I had to move quickly. You know this is right for my career. I'll make this work. I'm just being a crybaby for a minute."

I started thinking then that if I was going to move, I would have to give notice to my apartment. I might have been out of a job by the end of the week. Or I might be in jail. Either way, I realized I needed to start tearing things apart to put them back together down south. If I was confused before, I was even more conflicted then. Already, I felt at home at the MOL.

5

THE NEXT MORNING, I walked into the MOL like I had been a regular there for years. I said hi to Ivan, paid for my coffee, asked him the question I had been pondering as I showered and brushed my teeth, then headed for the back patio. I wanted to feel the quiet that the patio brought to me instead of all the thoughts that were running around in my brain. My thoughts felt like the five-year-old triplets I saw once in a curio store. They knew they had their parents outnumbered, so they took off in three different directions. One picked up a glass pumpkin and his mom took it from him while the dad tried to stop the second one from poking the shop cat with a back scratcher, and the third was trying to see if a letter opener would cut his finger. The triplets in my brain picked up and dropped my worries about my relationship with Isabella while poking at the conflicted feelings I was having about the job at Jason's company. I didn't know where the third triplet was, but I could hear something making suspicious noises in the corner of my brain.

Ivan came out with two cups in his hand. "Coffee with cream for you, oolong tea for me. Can I sit down?"

"Sure."

"Just a minute ago, you asked me if the questions on the wall will tell you how to find what's right for you in your life. The answer is yes, but with a caveat.

"Most of the people who come here have done a lot of reading and living and pondering in pursuit of the meaning of life, and after a lot of cups of coffee and a lot of discussion, we've decided that it's so different for each person that there isn't one correct answer. There's more of a place you go to find your answer, and those questions on the wall are big bright neon signs pointing toward that place. If you ask yourself those questions on a regular basis, you'll have a pretty good idea of what the meaning of life is for you, and where to find it.

"Over the course of your life, it'll change, of course, but the themes will remain the same. They'll be the themes of your life, lived on your terms, with you feeling satisfied each moment along the way that you're doing what you were meant to be doing. Your situation will change, or your needs will change, or your mind will change, but if you keep asking those questions you'll continue to be doing and living the life that's right for you in that moment."

He stopped for a second, took a drink of his tea, and watched a hummingbird sipping nectar from a wisteria flower. He waited another long moment before he started talking again.

"For a long time, who I was meant to be was a dad and husband. It took most of my time and thoughts and energy. During that time, the questions from the wall were like small wooden signs that marked a familiar path. I glanced at them as I went past, but there were no surprises, and they were just reminders for how to stay on that path.

"When the kids left, it was like the well-worn path through the woods changed into a series of roundabouts and forks on a highway that came at me quicker than I was used to. The words on the signs were the same, but they took on more meaning. They were still helping me to not feel lost, but the terrain was all new. I missed a few turns and doubled back quite a bit during that time, but I never felt completely without direction. I was able to navigate the twists and turns with the help of the questions."

He must have seen the confusion on my face because he stopped and looked at me expectantly. So, I asked him the question that was roiling inside me, "But how do you know who you were meant to be? That seems to be the biggest problem for me. I envy my friend who wanted to be a doctor his whole life because the path was so clear to him. Whenever he didn't know where to turn next, he thought to himself, 'What will move me toward being a doctor?' and then he did that. I have another friend who sets her sights on something and doesn't let anything get in her way until she achieves it. I'm not sure that's the answer for me either because she doesn't seem like she's enjoying what she's doing very much. She always seems like she's enduring what she's going through now because it will bring her to her goal in the end. She's happy when she reaches her goal. She's almost euphoric for a short while and then she goes through a tough time while she's looking for her next goal. The last goal had been her focus for so long that she doesn't know what to do next."

Ivan sat back in his chair. "Figuring out what you were meant to be is in many ways the easiest piece of the puzzle because you don't have to know any more than what you know right now. By examining yourself now, asking yourself what's important to you right now, and moving in that direction, you'll be moving toward who you were meant to be."

"I won't know who I am meant to be in the end, though. I'll only know what I can figure out right now. What if it changes?"

Ivan smiled a little. "Then change with it. That's the beauty of it. When you've moved toward what you can know right now, you'll see a little more, and you can adjust your direction. If you keep moving, you'll always be moving toward who you were meant to be. You have to have patience, and to believe that when you get as far as you can see, you'll have more clarity.

"If you ask the second question, too, you'll get even more clarity. Being a father suited me very well until the kids moved away, and then I started looking for changes to make. But even while I was on the set path of being a father, I asked myself those questions and made small changes to make sure I was living my best life as I could see it then. For instance, when my job started asking me to travel more, I enjoyed it for a while, but started to realize that I was putting off time with my kids for the money and excitement that the job was bringing. When I asked myself **If I died today,**

what would I regret? I kept coming up with the answer that I would be disappointed I hadn't spent more time with them when they were young. So, I changed direction. There was no need for a big change, but a minor course correction brought on by the questions kept me living the life that was right for me in the moment. The small choices we make and the moments that come from those choices add together to make a life."

6

WHEN I GOT TO work, I checked in with my boss before going to my office. "There's an agent from the SEC in your office now" he said, "He's going to need your passwords and any other help you can give him."

When I walked into my office, a dark-haired man was sitting at my desk, a cup of coffee in front of him, twirling his glasses absently in his left hand as he stared intently at my monitor. He looked up as I entered, and I introduced myself.

"I'm agent Klein. You can call me Calvin."

He saw my eyebrows raise and smiled. "Not really. I'm Ed, but I find that joke breaks the tension a bit."

"So, can you tell me what I'm supposed to have done? My boss dropped a bomb on me yesterday, but didn't really tell me anything, then told me to take the rest of the day off."

"First, let me ask you a couple of questions. Close that door behind you please. Do you have an account at Crescent Bank?"

"Sure. That's where the 401k is set up."

"Do you have a checking account there?"

"I don't think so. I signed a lot of paperwork my first day, but I didn't open one on purpose."

He looked at me seriously. "Well, you do have a checking account there. It looks like you set up a hidden function to apply a discount code to certain customer purchases, but instead of applying those discounts to the customer account, you moved the money into your checking account at Crescent Bank. It was well done. By taking money that neither the customer nor the company expected, nobody was looking for it. The code was well hidden too. Nice work."

"Except I didn't do it."

His expression got more menacing. "But yesterday after you left, you acted just like a fugitive would. You bought coffee, then a book, then later got pizza."

"You followed me?"

He grinned. "I'm messing with you. I've already been in your credit card account. Your password sheet's in your drawer. I could see what you bought yesterday."

"I know I didn't open an account or write that code, so someone must have set me up."

"I'm thinking the same thing. The person who wrote the code made it look like you did by using some of your shortcuts, and having the money go into an account in your name. You wouldn't be dumb enough to do that. I think they were waiting until the account was full enough and they could empty it and cover their tracks if nobody found it. Don't talk about this with anyone at work, but also don't stress too much. I'll be done here in a couple hours, and you can have your desk back."

Having a clear conscience doesn't mean I wasn't stressing about the bank account or what my boss said. So, I was relieved when agent Calvin Klein (I can't stop calling him that) told me he didn't think I was guilty, and my worry level dropped almost back to normal.

7

I STARTED PACKING UP my apartment that evening. Packing felt like something I could do because it took brainpower to decide what to keep and what to not take with me, and it was physical work. No matter what happened, I would have a cleaner apartment. In the middle of sorting a box of papers, a thought came to me.

Was I set up as a diversion, or was someone trying to make it look like I did something? Did someone set me up on purpose?

I went back to the papers. I had to read each one and decide to keep it or throw it away, and it kept those big questions further back in my mind. It also kept me from thinking about the weight of the decisions I had to make and what they would mean to me. After that,

I started making lists of what I needed to do before going to Los Angeles. I still had a couple of days before I had to break the news to my work and my landlord.

While I was packing, Isabella called. She told me her new job was still being tough. She didn't feel like she fit in yet, and she kept running into dead ends when she tried to get projects going the way she thought they should. She hadn't made any friends yet. She said she knew she would, but there was a nagging voice inside her saying maybe she wouldn't, and maybe she wasn't good enough to take on what she was being asked to do there.

It was the first time I had heard her have self-doubt. It was the first time she had told me about things that worried her. She was usually so invincible and so sure about where she was going. I felt closer to her than I had in a long time. I didn't try to fix anything, I just listened.

She asked if I was going to take the job at Jason's company and told me how great it would be to have me back in the same place with her. She told me how great the opportunity was. She told me she missed me. I told her I missed her too, but as soon as we hung up, I started thinking about what Ivan and I had talked about. Is she on the path toward who I'm meant to be?

8

THE NEXT MORNING, I left for work a half hour early so that I could spend more time in the coffee shop. Wispy tendrils of fog were blowing on a light cold wind, looking like smoke as they rounded the corners of buildings, so after ordering my coffee I turned into the living room where it would be warmer. A young woman in an oversized sweater was curled up on a large chair in the corner with her shoes on the floor and socked feet on the cushion. She had a cup in one hand and a book in the other. She looked up and said hi as I entered. I chose another overstuffed chair with a small wooden table next to it because it had a footstool and I love to put my feet up. I wasn't sure whether to take off my shoes then decided to because hers were off. I started back reading *Almost Everything* where I had stopped the day before.

When Ivan brought the coffee, he asked, "Have you two met? Sarah, Scott works in tech, and Scott, Sarah does too. You'll have to find out the rest of the answers yourselves."

I didn't feel like talking about what we did for work, so I jumped right in. "So, Sarah, what's your favorite question from the wall?"

She smiled. "Just the way I like to start a conversation. No small talk. Get right to what's important." She paused for a second and gazed up to the right as she thought. Her eyes were the same green as her sweater, emerald colored, like a still pond reflecting afternoon light from the surrounding trees. "You know, that's a question you could ask anyone if you wanted to skip the small talk. You could just dive in with 'What's important to you right now?' There would be no messing around with frivolities. So, my favorite question from the wall? It changes, but at this minute, I'm enjoying asking myself **Am I being kind?**"

"Why is that?"

"At first when I would ask that question, I was asking **am I being kind to other people?** Any time I was being kind to someone else, I felt like my life had meaning. Just by doing a kindness, I brought meaning with the action. It made me happier too. When I'm feeling down or feeling like I'm not going anywhere in my life, I can make myself happier by being kind to someone. It feels like when you give a present of a kindness to someone else, you're giving it to yourself too. Two birds with one stone. Although I never liked that saying. There should be a better one. Maybe picking two ripe peaches with one hand."

I raised my hand like I was in school. "Oh, or rescuing two kittens with a single net."

She chuckled. "Right. Or eating two flavors of ice cream at the same time. Anyway, giving kindness to someone else always seems to make me feel better too."

I leaned my elbow on the arm of the chair, so I was facing her more directly. "I hadn't thought about that. Does it work all the time?"

"It's pretty foolproof," she said, nodding, "If you're feeling down, do something to make someone else feel better, and you will too. But that's not why it's my favorite question right now."

"Then what makes it your favorite question?"

"I've started thinking of the question as, **Am I being kind to myself?** I think that as we move through life, we tend to be harder on ourselves than we are on others. We expect that we'll work through things and move forward a lot faster than we would expect others to. I find myself being mean to myself; Being impatient and saying cruel things to myself."

"Not being kind to yourself?"

She pushed a lock of her hair that had fallen in her face back behind her ear. "Yeah. For example, last week I set myself a goal of reading more and looking at my phone less. I wanted to start by bringing a book along with me in the morning so that if I had a spare moment, I could read instead of getting sucked into whatever my phone brought me. I left the house without the book, and when I realized it, the first thing I said was, 'What an idiot. I forgot the book. It was probably a stupid idea anyway.' Can you imagine if someone else said that to you? You wouldn't hang around them much. But we give that kind of abuse to ourselves all the time, and we take it from ourselves too, without really thinking it's wrong."

She sat up straighter and put her feet on the floor. "I think I might be talking too much."

"No, it's just right. I'm that way too. I'm so much tougher on myself than I would ever be with other people, and I say meaner things too. So, what did you do?"

"Luckily, I was being aware of being kind to myself, so I heard what I was saying. I stopped and took the chance to apologize to myself and to try again. I said, 'I didn't mean to say it like that. That sounded mean. What I meant to say was, I forgot the book. I'll remember it tomorrow. I can still not look at my phone, even if I don't have a book to read.'

I put my feet on the floor too, facing toward her. "But does being kind to yourself get in the way of getting things done? Sometimes the only way I get going is to kick myself in the pants. You know, 'Okay Scott, time to get out of bed and get some work done.'"

She smiled. "That didn't sound too mean."

"You're right. I get what you're saying. It's not the intent of the thing, it's how you say it, and what kind of a fuss you make of it. Like that last part before you restated what you said. When you said that it was a stupid idea. I do that to myself a lot. I even take it a step further and tell myself that I've screwed things up for the future. If I forgot the book, I might say, 'Well, I might as well give up on that idea. I'm not going to read more.'"

"Now that's mean."

We were quiet for a moment as I thought about what she had said. "Yeah. It has the effect of undermining what I'm trying to do. So, being kind to myself doesn't mean allowing myself to stay in bed all day, it's just treating myself as I would a friend instead of saying mean things to myself."

"Right, saying mean things to yourself that undermine what you really want."

I shook my head. "It's crazy that we would say things to ourselves that stop us from doing something we consciously want to do. How hard is it to change the way you talk to yourself?"

"I find it's mainly about being aware and being willing to take the time to go back and change what I said to myself. If I believe that what I say to myself is important I'll give it a little attention throughout the day. If I believe that it's worth changing, then I'll start saying different things to myself."

Right then, I became very aware of our surroundings. The warm room, comfortable colors and couches, her sitting directly across from me, intently interested in this deep conversation we were having. We didn't know each other, and we had jumped right in talking about things we cared about. I don't know if I've had this type of conversation in years, maybe ever. When I realized that, my first impulse was to make a joke, to lighten things up, but I didn't do it. I focused back on her and on what she had just said. I dragged my mind away from its attempt to get shallow and headed right back into the depths.

"Is there anything else that you're doing to be kind to yourself, or is talking to yourself differently the main part?"

She had been quiet while I wandered for a moment, and she smiled as I came back to the conversation. "Talking differently is the main part, but expectations are also mixed up in there somehow. I expect myself to magically make changes when I decide I will, and I get frustrated if they don't happen immediately. I have very little patience for the time it takes to accomplish what I want. I think the expectations may be harder to adjust, but at least I can stop berating myself when I don't reach my goals as quickly as I think I should."

"I read somewhere that it's okay if you don't always make the action or say the word that you intended to. Intentions are just that. The only judge you have is you, and you can be kind to yourself."

"I'm working on that. When I don't do what I planned, I'm starting to tell myself simply, 'I'll do it the next time.' It's so much kinder and gentler than getting mad at myself."

An idea popped into my head, and I bounced a little in my chair as I said it. "We need to treat ourselves like kids learning something new. We wouldn't yell at them; we would just give them encouragement and tell them to try again."

"Yes! We should treat ourselves as we would a six-year-old." She searched for words, then found them, "Kind, firm and supportive."

"And optimistic. We all expect that a six-year-old will learn eventually. We don't worry about how many tries it'll take."

She looked at the clock on the wall. "I have to go to work now but this has been great. When we started, I was the one talking about kindness, and between us we came up with a whole new set of ideas. Amazing. I'm often here in the mornings. I'll see you again."

"Yeah. I'd like that."

The sweater that had looked so comfortable and bunchy when she was sitting down fell neatly around her hips like a short dress as she stood up. I watched its rhythm as she left the room.

Sarah. What a nice person. Thoughtful too. I sat back in the easy chair, put my feet back up on the footstool, and looked around the room. The artwork on the walls was the kind that you could look at for a long time and not get tired of. One painting was about three feet square with random rounded squarish shapes in a mix of browns and beiges and blacks with blues and greens and reds sprinkled in. It was soothing and stimulating at the same time. My eyes relaxed while looking at it, but some part of my mind kept going back over it, looking for a pattern that never appeared. After thinking and worrying so much the past couple of days, it felt good to lose myself in the painting, without too many thoughts coming through.

I started to become aware of a warm feeling in my stomach. Was it because of the coffee, or was it the good conversation I had just had, or was it from the meditative effect of the painting? Maybe it was a combination of all three. I settled into the chair to read for a while before I had to go to work.

9

WHEN I SHOWED UP at work that day, it was like nothing had happened at all. Agent Klein was gone, my boss was in a meeting, and I had a pile of work to do, so I buckled down to get it taken care of. When I saw my boss later and asked him, he just said, "We'll get into that later."

10

AFTER WORK, I WENT out to the park for my weekly pick-up soccer game.

It always feels good to get out and run to clear the cobwebs from my brain, but that day there was more junk in there than usual, and every time I sprinted down field, I left more thoughts behind.

When I'm playing, I lose myself for a couple hours. No thoughts of the outside world make it through onto the playing field. They can't. The physical exertion and the immediacy of the game keeps my mind focused on what's in front of me, not on what might come later or what happened before. For a little while afterward, my mind stays clear too. I can go back to everyday life without thoughts jumping in and bouncing my emotions. I watch myself to see how long after playing I can stay in clear-headed game mind before I lose myself in everyday worries and thoughts again.

After the game, my buddy Alberto and I went for a beer. I like Alberto because he has a wide-open mind. You can say anything to him, no matter how crazy it sounds at first, and he'll think about it and ask a question to get more information. I could tell him that I think aliens landed on Chrissy Field last night, and he would pause and ask, "Why do you think that?" He's a sponge for information, but it's not all thrown together like rocks in a bucket. It's cross-referenced and categorized and tabbed so that we can be talking about cancer treatments, and he suddenly starts connecting that to airplane control systems and it make sense.

I told him about work and the bank account and diverting funds and asked him what he thought. "I bet it's your boss. Think about it. He had access to your ID when you were hired, so he could open an account in your name, but so did other people. But he knows what your coding looks like. He's the only one with both those pieces of knowledge. You should tell that to your buddy Calvin Klein. If it's him, he wouldn't be trying to set you up on purpose. He could do that in other ways. He was just trying to hide the money that he was diverting until he could move it somewhere else."

I was starting to think the same thing. It made me feel better if I thought that I just got caught up in my boss's scam, than that someone was out to get me.

Then I told him about the MOL. I told him about the questions on the wall, and Ivan and Sarah and the books and French press coffee and how it felt like such an inviting, comfortable place while still feeling stimulating and exciting.

He sat back and crossed his arms, lowering his chin a little as he looked at me. "Are you joining a cult?"

"No, it just feels like a place where I can learn things that I need to learn right now, with good people."

"Sounds kind of fishy. Your eyes are shiny, and you're all worked up like someone who's newly converted."

I was disappointed in his response, and I started backpedaling. "It's not like that. Nobody's trying to tell me what to do. They're just good people trying to live good lives."

"I just wonder what they're getting out of it. People don't open coffee shops on alleys where they won't make any money just for the general good of humanity."

I changed the subject. He wasn't responding like Alberto at all. We talked about sports for a while and then left.

I thought about what he had said as I walked home. The MOL didn't feel wrong. Nobody was trying to convert me, and nobody was trying to make money from me, except for coffee. The people seemed genuine, and there was a calmness about them that you don't find in just any group of random people.

But what was it that made Alberto act like that? What had he seen that I was missing?

11

THE NEXT DAY WHEN I smiled at the mole on the front window, opened the door, and breathed the aroma of coffee beans being ground, I almost ran into a woman who was straightening a picture on the wall by the door. After I apologized and stepped into the shop, she turned toward me and said, "You must be Scott. Ivan said you had started coming in at this time. I'm Audrey."

The first thing I noticed about Audrey was her kind face, with dark blue grey eyes like the ocean on a cloudy day. She looked straight at me for a long second, a small smile on her lips that finally spread to the corners of her eyes. In her face, I could see that she was predisposed to like me with my confusions and rough edges and missteps, and of course, I immediately liked her too because of the acceptance I saw there.

She moved toward the counter with the same strength and balance that showed in her face, making me think she must practice yoga. When she reached the counter, she turned to me and said, "Go find a place to sit and I'll make your coffee."

Fog was still blowing outside so I settled into the easy chair in the cozy room again. As Audrey set the coffee on the table by me, she asked me, "So, Scott, what's your favorite question from the wall?"

"I keep coming back to, **Am I moving toward who I'm meant to be?** It's something that's been troubling me. My job isn't very fulfilling to me. I keep feeling like I'm putting in time there instead of doing something that matters to me."

She sat on the overstuffed arm of the chair across from me. "And so?"

I picked up the cup, warming my hands on it. It was still too hot to drink. "So, I feel like I should be somewhere else, but I don't know where that is, or what it would look like in the end, and I don't know how to get started to go there since I don't know where there is anyway. I have an offer of another job, but I don't think I should just jump without having some idea of where I'm meant to be."

"That's what I love about that question." She scratched her chin, then continued. "It doesn't say, 'Am I who I'm meant to be?' It says, **Am I *moving toward* who I'm meant to be?** Movement is the key. Movement toward something. And sometimes movement away from what isn't working is as good as movement toward the right thing. A small decision to take a small action toward what you think might be right for you is the most important part. It's okay to change your mind throughout the process. What can you do that would give you a taste of what may be right for you?"

I blew on my coffee and took a small sip. Still too hot. "I can keep coming back here and exploring ideas and opening my mind to new thoughts. But what you're saying is that taking an action toward exploring what kind of work would be right for me is important." Then, nodding my head as something came to me, "Maybe I could talk with some people in careers I think might fit me better."

"That's positive movement. Exploring. I have a friend who runs a company that buys clean energy assets, windmills, solar farms and such, and runs them. Maybe you could talk to her. She feels like she's doing good in the world every day. It may not be right for you, but it would be one more idea to look at. What's right for you won't be right for someone else. I'm always amazed at what people love that I couldn't imagine myself doing."

She let herself slip from the arm of the chair into the chair, and leaned forward. "Let me tell you about my friend Todd. I've always been a person who strives for balance in my life, not working too late or letting it get in the way of other things I wanted to do, but that's not what works for other people.

"As long as I knew Todd, he worked too hard, but he loved it, I could tell. I used to own a construction company doing upgrades to office spaces, and Todd was one of my suppliers. We worked on a lot of projects together. We're almost the same age, but other than that we were opposites. Todd was tall and wide. He was once an offensive lineman in the NFL. Like Joan Rivers, his motto seemed to be, 'Enter the room talking.' He was always on the move, and always had an opinion.

"One Friday afternoon, I called him to ask a question about a project. As we spoke, I could hear forklifts in the background. Here's how the conversation went."

She held an imaginary phone to her ear. 'Todd, It's five o'clock. It sounds like you're still working.'

'It's six here, and I'm not going to be done until Monday.'

'Where are you?'

'Audrey, I'm in Phoenix. We're opening a new branch here. Grand Opening is Monday and I'm working all weekend.'

'Let me ask you something. Are you having fun?'

'I'm having a blast.'

'Is there anywhere else you'd rather be?'

'Nowhere. We're going a hundred miles an hour, and I'm loving it.'

'Are you putting anything off until later? Family, that sort of thing?'

'Not at all. My family and I just got back from a two-week vacation to visit my wife's relatives in Germany. We had so much quality time together.'

'Well, have fun.'

'I am buddy.'

She pushed the button to hang up her imaginary cell phone. "And here's the kicker. Todd died of a heart attack on New Year's Eve three months later. I was so glad I had asked him those questions because I was able to tell his wife at the funeral what I had asked him and how he had answered. What was right for Todd would have made me crazy, but it worked for him."

I looked at her for a couple of seconds, waiting to see if she had any more to say. Her eyes glistened, then she smiled and looked away.

I cleared my throat and looked into the corner for a second to give her time, then I said, "That story mixes up two of the three questions on the wall. **If I died today, what would I regret?** It sounds like Todd would be able to say he didn't regret much. Todd was living the life he was meant to be living. Not the one you would have chosen, but if he had asked himself, **Am I moving toward who I'm meant to be?** he probably would have had a positive answer."

She wiped something out of her eye. "The questions don't stand alone, do they? They lead into each other. If you're moving toward who you're meant to be, you probably would have fewer regrets."

My coffee was finally cool enough to drink, so I took a couple of sips. "Sarah and I were talking about kindness yesterday. She was exploring being kind to yourself as well as being kind to other people. Being kind to yourself is important as you move toward who you're meant to be."

"I agree, Scott, and supporting other people to move toward who they're meant to be requires kindness and understanding of them too."

She stood up. "I just thought of another **If I died today what would I regret?** story. Is that too much dying talk for one day?"

I smiled. "No, I think I can hear another."

"I'll tell you when I come back. It might be a couple of minutes."

When she returned, she had a cup of tea in one hand, and two carrot raisin muffins in the other. She handed me one of the muffins and sat down in the chair across from me again. "Spoiler alert. This one is about me, but I didn't die."

We both chuckled at her joke, and she continued. "I had graduated from college and was working and living at home while applying to graduate schools. I wanted to go to a ranked program, and most of them were on the east coast, so that was where I was applying.

"One day in the spring, a couple of friends and I went for a drive along the coast. One of them knew of a hidden beach above Santa Cruz and wanted to try to find it again.

"We parked by the side of the road, trekked on a dirt tractor path between rows of brussels sprouts plants to a cliff overlooking the ocean. Down a steep path sixty feet below was a cove with a sandy beach that looked like it was a scene from a movie. It was tiny, just an inlet, surrounded by cliffs, with a shark tooth shaped spire that looked like it had broken off the cliff jutting out of the waves in the center of the inlet. Off to the side of the cove, a dark shadow looked like it could be a cave, or an arch carved by waves.

"We climbed down the path to the cove, sometimes holding onto roots to keep from slipping. On the beach, it was warmer than it had been on the cliffs because it was protected from the wind. We explored the cave, played in the waves, ate salami and cheese and bread we had brought, and drank some wine.

"Then one of the guys suggested that we try to climb the spire in the middle of the cove. I'm a careful person, and the spire looked steep but climbable, but the only reason I agreed was that the water was four feet deep under the side we would try to climb. I figured if we fell off, we wouldn't get hurt too badly.

"We waded out into the waves and started climbing the rock face. As I climbed up, there were a couple of dicey moments maneuvering around outcroppings.

"We stayed on top for a couple of hours, enjoying the sun and the view, then we started to climb down. When I looked over the edge, I realized that the tide had gone out, and the four feet of water that I had depended on as my safety net on the way up had disappeared. The area under our climb was now hard wet sand, with an occasional wave lapping at it.

"I went first. The outcroppings that were hard to get around on the way up were harder on the way down, and scarier because I knew there was no water under us this time. I didn't mention it to my friends, but I was worried. One of them lost his footing and started to slide down toward me. I had a firm hold on a bush and was able to grab his shorts at the waist to slow him enough that he could get his footing again.

"As I was going around one outcropping, a piece of rock came loose in my hand, and I almost lost my balance. I couldn't help thinking about the hard sand below.

"We got to the bottom, and everyone was fine, and we continued with our day. I had been scared, but I'm not sure everyone else was as worried as I had been."

She paused to take a bite of her muffin and sip her tea. "It wasn't until that evening, sitting on the couch with my grandmother, who was living with us because of her health, that I started to cry. She asked me what was wrong, and I realized that if I had fallen off that cliff, I would have missed the time we were able to spend together that year. I loved being able to talk with her between all the things I was doing.

"That made me think again about my plan to go away for graduate school. Doing that would have made me miss time with her, and I knew that her time was limited. I changed where I was applying to school so I could spend more time with her and ended up going to school close to home."

I had finished my muffin and was wondering if she was going to finish hers as she continued. "It took a scare on a cliff to make me realize how important she was to me and how much I valued the time we spent together. I didn't have to ask the question, **If I died today, what would I regret?** in a circumstantial way. I really felt that I might have died, and the question hit me harder because of it.

"Someone else might have made a different decision but asking that question kept me on the path of what was right for me."

We sat in silence for a second, reflecting, then I spoke. "That's a beautiful story. Scary and beautiful. That was a big decision, deciding to stay local for grad school."

She saw me looking at her muffin and handed it over to me.

I took a deep breath and let it out slowly. "I'm facing a big decision in my life. I was offered a job in Los Angeles, with a lot more money and stress, near my girlfriend, Isabella, and I have to decide this week. I need to make changes in my life, but are those the changes I should be making? Would I be moving toward who I'm meant to be, or is my ego pushing me to take the job down there? It would be a step up in pay and responsibilities, and the company is one that everybody recognizes. Nobody knows the company I work at now. But do I want that? See?" I said, smiling wryly, "Already, the questions on the wall are helping me."

She nodded. "That's what we all have to answer for ourselves. I'm sorry that you haven't had the chance to experience small decisions using the questions on the wall before this huge decision, actually decisions, came up."

I sat quietly thinking about those decisions as Audrey waited. I started talking, almost to myself. "Isabella decided to move to LA because the move would be good for her career. It doesn't surprise me that she decided on her own because that's how she is. But she has so many good qualities. She's smart and she's strong, and I like the way she laughs, and we laugh together a lot. But she's not very happy within herself, and she doesn't want to explore ways to be happier with her life. She's not very comfortable talking about things that she can't see. When she's pursuing a goal, which she is almost all the time, she's very single-minded, Selfish."

I stopped, surprised at what I had just said. "Wow, that just popped out. I guess I think that her single-minded pursuit of her goals is kind of selfish. She certainly didn't think about me very much when she moved to LA."

I turned back toward Audrey, slightly embarrassed that I had been off in a world of my own for a minute, while still talking out loud, but she didn't seem bothered at all. "So, Audrey, what's the secret to a good relationship? I haven't seen you two together, but you and Ivan seem like such balanced people, and you've been married for a long time."

She didn't hesitate. She had obviously done a lot of thinking about that subject. "I guess it's a part of the first question. **Am I moving toward who I'm meant to be?** You could add on the corollary, **Am I supporting others to move toward who they're meant to be?**

"That's the most important part of a successful relationship, I think. If we support each other's growth and interests, we're like two trees in a forest with roots that intertwine and provide nourishment to the other without having to compete for the sunlight. And, as we figured out just now, the questions on the wall work together too. **Am I being kind?** That's part of supporting each other in our growth. Without kindness and tolerance, it's hard to have a successful relationship where each person is free to find their own path."

12

THAT NIGHT ISABELLA CALLED, and I told her right away that I wasn't going to take the job with Jason's company. My job wasn't right for me, and I could have been fired, but I probably wasn't going to jail, and the new one didn't sound like a good fit for me.

I told her I wanted to break up too, more than just geographically. She had moved away physically, but in the time she had been gone I had moved away emotionally.

When she moved, some part of her must have thought I would be pulled along by the force of her decisions, floating in her wake like leaves behind a semi-truck rushing along the freeway.

After our breakup talk, I felt light initially, but all that evening and the next morning too I felt a weight on the back of my neck. I felt sad for her and for us, because there were so many good things we had shared. I had loved her, and I would miss her, but what Audrey said about the best relationships consisting of supporting the other person to be who they're meant to be had rung true with me.

I told her that when she asked why. I told her that I felt I was caught up in her stampeding herd of horses, knowing that running with her could be exhilarating but also knowing that if I didn't run, I could be trampled or left behind. I told her I needed someone who would run with my herd sometimes, or at least notice that my herd isn't always running in the same direction hers is.

She didn't say she could change. She knows herself well enough for that. But damn, she's having a hard time in her new job, and it would be so much easier for her if I were there. I liked being part of her herd. I felt like I was letting her down by not going.

I felt sad, but it wasn't a sharp sadness, more like a memory of a loss that had occurred a while ago. Some part of me felt like the breakup happened when she moved to Los Angeles, and I had finally realized it that night. It didn't feel new and raw. It felt more like something that had been going on for a while in the background, and I had finally looked at it and acted on it just then.

13

THE NEXT MORNING, AS I opened the door to the MOL, I hoped Audrey would be there. I wanted to ask her more questions. Breaking up with Isabella had left me worn out that night, but in the morning, it seemed like having made a decision opened up space in my mind for new and exciting thoughts to flood in.

She was there, behind the counter, reading. As I paid for my coffee, I asked her a question. "How is it that everyone here seems so balanced? It seems like you're exactly where you want to be, without the angst and dread that I keep feeling."

She smiled at me. "You haven't even had coffee yet, and already your mind is racing. Let me catch up. I'll make the coffee and meet you in back."

I was examining one of the other paintings in the living room up close when she came in. "I love that one. I could look at it forever, I think."

We sat down in the same chairs as the prior day, and she started to answer my question. "I think the balance comes from going back to the questions, especially the first one. **Am I moving toward who I'm meant to be?** The second part of that balance you're sensing is acceptance of where we are, and acceptance that we can't know all the answers right now, and that's okay. It's not an effortless balance though, any more than riding a bike is effortless. Riding a bike is about always being a little unbalanced and making a small correction to bring that balance back. Even turning is an odd combination of first turning the handlebars the wrong direction to cause unbalance, then leaning and turning in the right direction." She tilted her head and looked at a painting on the wall for a second before starting again. "I like that metaphor. On a bike or in life, a turn in the wrong direction can be the start of another turn in the right direction.

"Then we return to the idea that we can't see any further than what's in front of us right now, so if we've done everything we can as best we know, we can relax and enjoy where we are. I think that feeling of being balanced comes from having resolved the conflicts that we can know and accepting the rest."

I sipped my coffee and leaned toward her. "I just had an image pop into my head of my brothers and me playing sports. I was the youngest of three boys, and we were close in age, just a couple of years between each of us. Being the youngest, I was always trying to keep up with my brothers. Because of that, I played with an intensity that neither of them had. I had to, to keep up. When I was in the middle of a game, I was fierce. I loved it. I was smiling the whole time I was playing, but I was all in. Then when the game was over, I left it behind." I put my hand above my head, at the height of a taller person. "My next older brother often cried when he lost, and the oldest one seemed to use each loss as a brick in a wall of resentment that would strengthen him for the next time. He seemed to draw on past losses to propel him into intensity in the next game.

"I just had fun. I turned off the whole world and competed with everything I had, then when the game was over, I marked down the score on my mental scorecard and then threw the scorecard away."

I scratched my head as I thought for a moment. "I had a coach say to me once. 'Scott, you know what your problem is? You don't care if you win or lose.

You're smiling and joking after a loss. We can't have that attitude. If you don't hate losing, you'll allow it to happen to you, and that's unacceptable.' I believed him for a while and pasted a frown on my face, but that lasted about one game. I just couldn't harbor the pain of a loss or the elation of a win for very long.

"Maybe it was what you said about resolving the conflicts we can know and accepting the rest. That's what it felt like for me when the game was over. It was done, and I had resolved everything I could. The outcome was the outcome. I couldn't get worked up over something that had already happened. Is that acceptance?"

She nodded her head. "Sounds like it to me. Where else does that show up for you?"

I looked up toward the ceiling, then wondered why people do that. Sarah had done that the other day. It seems like the place you look for deep thoughts is in the right corner of the room. I looked up there for another beat as a thought came to me. "My parents used to say I was raised by wolves. I spent a lot of time following my brothers, trying to keep up. Maybe those were the wolves that raised me. My wolfpack of brothers, wrestling and running and bumping me back into line, without a lot of talking going on. And, by the time I came along, my parents had decided that it was better if kids made a lot of mistakes early and figured out for themselves what was right and wrong. But spending a lot of time as the youngest one at the tail end of the wolf pack meant a lot of things were out of my control, and I had to accept them if I wanted to hang with the pack. And I did want to hang with the pack. More than anything. I hadn't realized it until now, but I don't have that in my life now. I miss that. Hanging with the pack. I'll have to think about that. Where could I get that feeling in what I'm doing now?"

I thought about that all the way to work, hardly noticing where I was walking as I replayed the conversation with Audrey in my head.

14

IN THE MIDDLE OF the morning, deep in a spreadsheet, I found myself thinking of my friend who's in medical school. I stopped cutting and pasting numbers and gave that thought my attention. He told me that his dad sat him down before he left for his first year of school and gave him some advice. He thought it must be important because his dad almost never gave him advice.

His dad said, "You're starting on a path that will take eight or ten years of hard work. I recommend that you think of those years as part of your life and find enjoyment in them as they happen. If you think of this time as something you're doing that will bring you to the start of your real life and happiness at the end of it, you will have paid for your degree with all those years of unhappiness. Remember, this is your life. Your life is happening now. Enjoy it now, however you can, even the long hours and hard work."

It's not just my friend. My life is happening now. If I'm somewhere, I need to accept it and enjoy it, or start to change it. Then it struck me. I can enjoy it while I change it. I don't have to hate it to change it, I just need to know that it's not taking me where I'm meant to be. It's like what Audrey said about riding a bike. I'm always making small corrections and course adjustments while riding a bike, but it's part of the experience. I can still feel the wind in my face and love the view as I make changes. And like riding a bike, I'm always the one deciding where to go.

15

AS I TURNED DOWN the alley the next morning, I saw Sarah. I didn't know it was her at first. I saw a woman standing in the sunlight, turned sideways to me. Her auburn hair looked almost red in the morning light. She was talking with someone on her phone. She finished the call as I walked up, looked at me and smiled.

I smiled back and said, "You look like someone I'd like to hang out with. Want to go somewhere for a cup of coffee?"

She gave me a wry grin. "I don't know. Where would we go?"

"Oh, I know a place."

She narrowed her eyes. "Yeah, but you look kind of dangerous. Are you trustworthy?"

"Grandmothers and small children like me."

"Good enough references for me. I'm buying."

We walked together to the MOL, ordered coffee, and headed to the back patio. There was a guy sitting at one of the tables. She got a big smile on her face, said, "Hi Gary," and went over to give him a hug.

Okay, this wasn't just a guy. He was a hunk. That's the one-word description. Here's a few more words. Handsome. Chiseled. Hubba-hubba. I'm a straight guy and I thought Hubba-hubba.

Then I realized I was feeling suddenly feeling sad. I mean depressed sad. I realized I had looked at them together and thought to myself, *Well, they're a couple. You have no chance with her. Might as well keep packing your things.*

I didn't have time to think about it more because she called me over and introduced us. "Scott, meet Gary. I think you guys will like each other."

Does she think I'm gay? Is he gay? I felt better already. *Maybe he is gay.*

He was still standing, and I put out my hand and we shook hands. "Hi Gary. Did you and Sarah meet here?"

"Yeah. My wife, Hope, and I have been coming here for a long time."

Wife? Yes! Mental fist pump, like when Tiger Woods sinks a putt.

I returned my attention to what he was saying. "It just feels right here. I love the combination of the patio and the cozy living room, and everyone who comes here is interesting in one way or another. They're people who are intentional with their lives. They think about things and do things and then they think about them some more. You would imagine that all that reflection would keep them from getting out and doing something, but it's the opposite. People here move strongly in the world. Maybe it's because they don't get in their own way as much as most people." He paused and looked at Sarah and me. "Did you guys meet here?"

Does he think we're a couple? Do we look like we are?

The memory of her sitting on the cozy chair, feet tucked under her came into my head. "Yeah, just the other day." I smiled at the memory, then turned my attention back to him. "I get what you're saying about moving in the world. Since I've been coming here, I've gotten more clarity on where I should be going. It makes it easier to move when you have some internal guidance, and the questions help. What's your take on the questions?"

He reached down to the table for his coffee and took a sip before answering. "I've started to use them to figure out what I want my future to feel like instead of what I want it to be like. I can visualize the feelings I want to have in my life easier than I can imagine the circumstances that might lead to those feelings. Then when I find the circumstances that match the feelings I want to head for, I know they're right."

My phone buzzed in my pocket, and I reached in to silence it. "Feelings instead of circumstances. What do you mean by that?"

"Well, we were just talking about the MOL." He opened his hands and looked around, indicating the patio. "Before we found this, we imagined it. Hope and I talked about how it's hard to make friends that you can talk about important subjects with. We started imagining where we could meet people like that. We came up with a scenario made up of feelings. It would be a warm place, with books, and with people coming and going who enjoyed conversation and reading. It wouldn't be quite like a library because those are too quiet and wouldn't be like a bookstore because there's not enough room to sit around. We imagined the people too. We thought of who we had known that we wanted to hang around with more and imagined those people in that space. Then, when we found the

MOL, we knew. It wasn't exactly like anything we had imagined, but it felt like a mix of all we had imagined. The feelings were a guide."

I nodded in agreement. "I was just doing that yesterday when I was talking about my brothers and me. We were like a wolfpack, kind of a non-verbal knowledge that we had each other's backs and could spend a lot of time together without having to talk a lot. There was a closeness that came from that too. As I talked about it, I realized I missed that feeling. So, that could be a better guide than trying to recreate a family of brothers wrestling with each other. I could think about the feelings I got from that and recognize it when it shows up in another way."

Sarah had backed off a step as we spoke, and was standing watching us, listening, with her arms crossed and a bemused smile on her face. She looked like a different person when she smiled like that. With each emotion, her face changed. She let so much of her emotions show and they showed everywhere on her face. Thoughtful Sarah looked more like a cousin of bemused Sarah than the same person with a different expression. Like the painting inside the MOL with the rectangles and squares and browns and blues, you could look for a long time and not find all the answers.

Gary's voice broke through my thoughts. "Hey, do you guys want to go to a Giants game tomorrow night? I have four tickets. You could come with Hope and me."

I looked at Sarah. She nodded. "Sure. We'd love to." I felt something jump in my stomach. Optimism?

16

WE MET IN FRONT of the stadium, at the statue of Willie Mays captured in bronze as he watches a home run go over the fence, bat behind him touching the ground at the end of his swing. We got there early so we could wander around the stadium and get some food before the game started. We each had a backpack with extra sweatshirts and windbreakers and gloves and stocking caps. We aren't tourists. We live here. We know. You can always tell a tourist in San Francisco in the summer by their shorts, and the hurriedly purchased souvenir sweatshirt with the hood up. At a baseball game, they always leave early.

Hope and Gary wanted to try the crab sandwiches, so we headed toward centerfield by the huge sculpture of an old fashioned puffy leather baseball glove, upright, ready to catch a fly ball as big as the moon.

I hate to go to a baseball game and not get a hotdog and a beer, but there's hotdog stands all over the park, so I followed along. Sarah got nachos. When I told her they looked good, she said she would trade me some for some of my food.

When we got to our seats, which were about ten rows above the visitor's dugout on the first base line behind the foul net, Hope said, "Wow, nice seats. Not like the last time we came." She shaded her eyes and looked off into the distance. "Those were the type of seats where you say, 'I can see our car from here. I think we left the lights on.'"

We laughed, and Sarah started telling a story. "I went to an A's game with my uncle and my dad and my brother when I was a kid. My uncle was a huge A's fan and had gone to all the games during the years in the 70's when they won three world series in a row, with Catfish Hunter and Sal Bando and Reggie Jackson. We had to get there hours early so we could watch batting practice. He was so excited to get in that we had to run to keep up with him across the parking lot."

She scooped up a nacho and stuffed it in her mouth. As she chewed, she continued the story. "So, we got our food and sat in our seats, like today, and Mark McGuire was taking batting practice and hitting bombs out of the park, and the PA announcer said, 'Will the owner of a grey Plymouth minivan' and we looked at each other. We came in a grey Plymouth minivan."

She said it in that booming, echoing voice that PA announcers used to make. "Will the owner of a grey Plymouth minivan License number GNY264 please return to your car.' My uncle said, 'That's our car.' 'Will the owner of the grey Plymouth minivan please return to your car; you left the engine running.' My dad couldn't stop laughing. My uncle had been so excited to see the ball game that he forgot to turn off the engine. He said, 'We're not going to have enough gas to get home' and took off running up the steps. My dad called him Gas Hog the rest of the game. He tried at the next family dinner to get the name to stick, but my grandma put that idea to rest. 'John, he's a grown man. You can't go around calling a grown man Gas Hog.' After that, it was only his baseball game name. Hey Gas Hog, you want another beer? Hey Gas Hog, can I have one of your fries?"

Here's an idea I'm working on, and I'll just toss it out there because it seemed so real to me hanging out and laughing with them at the ball game that night. I read that the best way to improve your relationship with someone is to tell them that you love them just the way they are. It's hard to find the place to fit that in, though, with friends. With a partner, there are moments of quiet intimacy where it seems right to say something like that, but with friends, it has to come out another way.

It did that night. I felt like we were all saying to each other, "I'm an idiot in my own special way. Let me tell you about it." Hope told a story about how she left her car running overnight, and I told about the time I got fired, because that was on my mind, and Gary told about the time he pooped his pants when he was visiting Hope's parents' house for the first time. Sarah told us how she had, just the week before, called her boss Mom, and then made it worse by laughing so hard she snorted.

We were all letting the others see something we were embarrassed about and admitting that we were idiots, and it felt like we were all saying to the person who said it, "I like you partly because you're an idiot. Aren't we all?" There's a cozy camaraderie that arises from acknowledging that we're all messy imperfect idiots who make big mistakes and have insecurities and those insecurities sometimes (often) come out when we least expect them to and if our friends can laugh and call us Gas Hog, it makes the whole thing seem better.

17

ALBERTO TEXTED ME DURING the game. We talked the next morning. He told me about how his parents had gotten involved with a large church after he had gone to college. He said they had a different look about them when he came home for Christmas that year. He said they were suddenly very sure of things and had a faraway look in their eyes. When he saw me excited about the MOL, it brought that back, and also brought back memories of the trouble that had come with their fanaticism. He knew they were enthralled with the preacher and his teachings, and were getting more and more involved at the church, but didn't know how much until the next time he came home on break, and they were preparing to sell their house to fund a mission the church was going on.

He said he barely was able to talk them into not selling. They had already given a huge percentage of their savings to the church, but they kept the house. Not long afterward, the preacher disappeared, and nobody was able to say for sure where the money had gone. The strange thing was that his parents still believed in the preacher. They thought he would show back up and tell them all the good things that he had been doing with their money.

When he heard me talking about the MOL, and saw the excitement as I talked about it, he had flashed back to his parents without knowing exactly what he was thinking. Then he let me know that he didn't really think the MOL was a cult when he said, "And they're probably not trying to cheat you out of your student loan debt, so that's one less thing you have to worry about."

I asked him if he wanted to go there with me one day. He said he would meet me there later that morning.

18

WHEN I WALKED INTO the patio at the MOL, Alberto was standing by a table, coffee cup in one hand, gesturing toward the sky with the other, talking to a seated man I didn't know.

I heard Alberto saying, "It's not a question of what to do with your life that most people have problems with, it's a question of doing what they say. Lots of people will tell you they want something in their life, then do the opposite. Cognitive Dissonance. That's what I call it. They'll say, 'I wish I had more time to draw and paint' then they'll binge watch a show on Netflix. The question on the wall is right on point because it says **Am I moving toward who I'm meant to be?** It doesn't say, 'Am I pining for something I'm not willing to put in a little bit of work for?' It doesn't say,

Am I moving in a direction exactly opposite of what I say I want in my life?' or 'Am I sitting in my room making excuses for why things aren't working out for me while I'm not moving at all?' It talks about moving toward what you want for who you are and who you want to be. What I can't understand is why people do that. Why do they do the opposite of what they say they want?"

I spoke for the first time. "Fear."

Alberto looked over at me. "Fear?"

"I think that's it," I answered, "Fear of failure, fear that you're headed in the wrong direction and won't be able to get back if you go too far, fear that you're not good enough, fear for the sake of fear stopping you just because it makes you feel bad so you back away from where you thought you wanted to go."

Alberto looked at me like he didn't quite believe me. "Don't you just push through it?"

I shrugged. "Not all the time. Not me."

I looked down at the man. He was in his sixties, blonde hair going grey, thin, wiry. I would call him dapper because of his demeanor and cane and felt hat, but I was pretty sure he could drink and swear with the best of them. There was a toughness about him, and you can't call someone dapper if they can drink and swear and possibly beat you up.

I stuck out my hand. "Hi, my name is Scott."

Standing up and grabbing my hand, he said, "Dennis. Glad to meet you. Do you know Alberto?"

I squinted, pretended I was spitting on Alberto's shoes, and made a fist and held it out in front of me. "No, and there's something about him that I don't like. Makes me want to fight him." Then I smiled. "Yeah, we go back a ways."

Dennis sat back down. "So, Scott, fear? What about that?"

"I just started reading a book by the woman who wrote *Eat, Pray, Love*. Elizabeth Gilbert. It's called *Big Magic*. She talks about fear of failure or not being good enough stopping us from moving toward the things we want in our lives. It was able to stop her from writing when it got strong enough.

"She said when she started to realize that fear is part of anything important, which for her was creativity, she started to consciously invite fear to come along when she started something new. She would talk to it, telling fear that it was allowed on the road trip with her and her creative venture, but she and creativity were in the front seat, and fear had to sit in the back seat, and it wasn't allowed to choose where they were going. If it had to speak up it could, but it wasn't allowed to influence her decisions."

Alberto nodded. "By inviting fear along for the ride, she acknowledged that it was going to be there, but didn't let it rule her."

"Yeah, kind of like accepting it," Dennis said slowly, "It was going to be there, so she stopped running away from it or fighting it or trying to find a place where she could hide from it. She looked it in the eye and told it she wasn't afraid of it anymore."

Alberto pulled up a chair. "Sounds like she wasn't afraid of fear anymore. She wasn't trying to be tougher than it like I do. I just bully through even though it makes me sweat. She was tougher than me in a way because she was able to look it in the eye, pat the seat behind her, and say 'It's going to be a long ride. Climb in, here are the rules."

I said, "Reminds me of a Louis L'Amour novel. His characters are always the toughest guys around, and they know they are, so they don't have to show it. Sometimes someone tries to pick a fight with him, and he just smiles and gives them a way out so they can save face. He knows he's tougher than they are so he can cut them a little slack. I can imagine one of his characters saying, 'It's going to be a long trip, Fear. Saddle that bronco, and ride behind the herd to keep them moving. I'll be in front, scouting the trail."

I sat down at the table with them. "So, Alberto punches his way through the fear. I push through it most of the time, Elizabeth Gilbert invites it in, and lives with it but not comfortably. What do you do Dennis?"

He rubbed his eyes, then looked at me a bit ruefully. "I would have to say I wear it out. I guess it's a mix of the strategies. I know it's there, and I know it makes me uncomfortable, but I just keep trudging. Pretty soon it lets up. It never feels like I'm moving very fast or very far, but each day I get up and acknowledge the fear, knowing I might be completely lost and blind, then go ahead and get something done."

He put his fingers in front of his mouth like he was holding a cigarette there, and breathed in, through the upper knuckle, like a cowboy. It made me think he must have been a smoker at one time. "Some days it isn't much, but most days it's something. I talk to myself too. I tell myself I know I might be heading in the wrong direction like fear says, or I might be a total idiot, but until I find out for sure, I have to move in the direction I think is right as far as I can tell."

"I talk to myself a lot too." I said, "Every time fear tries to tell me something that's not in my best interests, I talk back to it. I tell it why it's not right. I tell it I have to keep moving."

Dennis sat forward in his chair. "It sounds like we have something in common even though we take different approaches. We keep moving, for the most part."

Alberto nodded his head. "You're right. Moving. **Am I moving toward who I'm meant to be?** Now that I think about it, procrastination might not be as much about being lazy as being afraid to move. When I find myself procrastinating about something I know I should be doing, I stop to figure out why. Usually, I find that I'm scared of something, or anxious that I might be headed in the wrong direction. I can get myself moving by telling myself to just take a small step and see what happens next. It makes me have a bit more understanding of why someone might say something and do another. They might have some fear that they're not pushing through one step at a time, however that works for them."

I nodded. "Yeah, one step at a time." I paused as another thought came into my head. "It's like going to the gym. When I don't want to go, I tell myself I'm just going to go and do a light, easy workout. That gets me there, and pretty soon I find myself pushing as hard as ever. Just showing up is most of the work."

<h1 style="text-align:center">19</h1>

MY BOSS WASN'T AT work that day. Whispered conversations around the office suggested that he had been fired, but nobody knew why. The word was he had been walked out the door by security. People were speculating about what he'd done, and somebody remembered that there had been a strange man in my office one day. When they asked, I just said he was using my computer for a couple hours, but I didn't know why. I had felt better after talking to Agent Klein, but this really closed the door on my worries about being in trouble at work. Now I had to figure out what I wanted to do, but I had time to give it some real thought.

20

I WENT BACK TO the MOL at lunch that day. Audrey wasn't there. I was hoping she would be because I had another thought about her bicycle analogy. I wanted to tell her that bikes are hard to ride if you're standing still. You really need to be moving or you fall over.

I would tell her the next time. I got a cup of Ivan's Oolong Tea to go.

I was walking out the door as Sarah came in. We talked for a minute, then I asked her if she wanted to go see the Georgia O'Keeffe exhibit at the Legion of Honor Museum. She said she had been wanting to see the show, and we made plans to meet there.

21

WE MET THERE ON the following Saturday just before it opened, in the parking lot perched on top of a hill looking at the golden gate bridge from the ocean side.

The exhibit was full of magnificent paintings of mountain and lake views in bright colors looking like they're in bloom, alongside close ups of flowers that don't look like flowers but instead like landscapes and mountains.

We didn't try to see anything other than that exhibit, then went to get breakfast in the museum cafe, feeling satisfied by the paintings and ravenous at the same time.

We walked downhill from the museum toward the ocean on a dirt path and found a labyrinth of small rocks on a cliff above the ocean. Not a maze, but a circular meditation path maybe fifty feet in diameter that winds back upon itself with one entrance and one way to the center and then one way back out. Neither of us had walked a labyrinth but we had heard of them, and we both wanted to try it. The turning and careful stepping made it so that by the time we reached the center, we felt very quiet, inside and out, like that quiet space I get after playing soccer. We smiled at each other and started back through the winding pathway to the exit. When we got out, neither of us felt like talking. We stood, side by side, looking across at the cliffs on the other side of the bay and at the seagulls with wings lifted on the breeze. I reached for her hand, and we stood looking out over the ocean for a long time.

22

ON MONDAY WHEN I opened the front door to the warmth and welcoming aroma of the MOL, Audrey was behind the counter. She commented that I looked calmer than I had been. I thought for a second, and replied, "You know, I've been taking care of a few things. I found this cool place called the MOL where there are thoughtful, kind people, and questions on the wall that help me to sort out where I'm going in my life. It makes things easier when you have a direction, and it feels natural when the direction comes from what's true inside not from what someone else thinks, or what you think the world thinks you should be doing."

She smiled a little as she poured the water over my coffee.

I continued. "The whole idea of acceptance of what you can't change has taken a lot of weight off my mind too. I'm worrying less. I take care of what I can, then let the rest go past me more. Of course, I'm just a beginner at that. It seems like there will always be something I can learn."

She handed me my cup of coffee, and replied, "That is the beauty of it, isn't it? We'll never run out of things to learn. It's exciting."

We both turned our heads as a guy about my age walked into the shop, making the bell ring as he opened the door.

He looked worried, and in a bit of a hurry. "Hi, can I get a cup of coffee? I'm a little lost. I was looking for something else and stumbled into this alley."

I gave Audrey a knowing nod and said, "I'll take my coffee to the back."

As I was heading down the hallway, I heard Audrey ask him, "You have time to drink it here?"

23

AS I SETTLED MYSELF into an easy chair, kicked off my shoes, put my feet up on the footstool, and took a first tentative sip of coffee, I thought back over the past couple weeks. I had found a series of questions that functioned as signposts to help me figure out where I was going in my life. I had used the insights from what I figured out to make changes in my life. Some had been big changes, ones that had been put off for too long, and some had been small, but all had been movements toward who I'm meant to be as I could see it from where I was.

And I was doing it while being kind to myself, not expecting too much to happen in any one moment, just knowing that showing up regularly gets you most of the way to where you want to be.

And I was starting to face fear knowing that I'm tougher than I think I am, and look it in the eye, and tell it to saddle a bronc and head out behind the herd.

And I had met so many thoughtful and kind people who are moving forward in the world with intention and purpose, and so much of it comes from the direction given by the questions on the wall. Audrey, who liked me immediately, and who was at that moment helping another lost person to start looking inside for guidance. Ivan, wise and quiet, a rock. Gary and Hope, vulnerable and able to laugh at the absurdity of who we are. And Sarah, warm, funny, wickedly smart, with facets to her personality that kept surprising and delighting me.

And the thought came to me that things were going to work out just fine.

But I know everything's not going to be rosy all the time. Life isn't like that. There's no "Happily ever after." Things happen, good and bad. That's what makes life interesting. All those moments, strung together, make a life.

But I'm learning that if I ask myself the three questions on the wall of the MOL Coffee Shop, my moments string together more smoothly in a way that works for me now, and look, when I take a the time to look back over them, almost like I had a plan; almost like I knew where I was going all along.

24

OH, AND ONE MORE thing. It turns out that from the direction I came upon the MOL there's a network of alleys where old streets were rebuilt after the 1906 earthquake. They run at slight angles to the main streets, between the buildings, relics of a time past when streets didn't always run in such straight lines and weren't very wide. They act as a funnel of sorts, each one intersecting with others and guiding you toward the alley where the MOL is, like branches on a tree. Almost anywhere you turn, if you kind of know the direction you're going, you end up at the MOL.

And that's not the craziest part. The end of the alley that I saw ahead of me, just before I decided to go in through the front door of the MOL on that glorious San Francisco day when I thought I might end up in jail and had no idea what to do next? That alley opens on the street I had walked up every day on my way to work. I had passed it thousands of times and not noticed.

The wall of the alley, as seen from the street, has bookshelves and a table with two steaming cups of coffee painted on it. In the middle of the bookshelves, visible from the street, at eye level, is a fat arrow pointing down the alley toward the MOL. In the middle of the arrow are block capital letters that say MEANING OF LIFE.

It just goes to show that the easy way isn't the only way to find who you're meant to be. You can wander through alleys, feeling lost, deciding which way to turn, depending only on the knowledge you have in the moment, and if you keep moving, you'll probably be going toward who you're meant to be, but unless you're looking, you'll probably walk right on by the signs that point you in the right direction.

***

Am I moving toward who I'm meant to be?
If I died today, what would I regret?
Am I being kind?

SOME OF THE BOOKS in the MOL Coffee Shop Bookstore:

Siddhartha

Conversations With God

Man's search for meaning

The Power of Now

Daring Greatly

Flow

Almost Everything

Loving What Is

The 7 Habits of Highly Effective People

Big Magic

The Road Less Traveled

Stitches

Quiet

The Gifts of Imperfection

Learned Optimism

Oh, the Places You'll Go

Mindset

Zen and the Art of Motorcycle Maintenance

The Art of Happiness

The Razor's Edge

Johnathan Livingston Seagull

Peace Is Every Step

Meditations by Marcus Aurelius

Stillness Speaks

VISIT OUR WEBSITE TO see other books by Matt Tracy

https://www.matttracyauthor.com/

ALSO BY MATT TRACY

Happy Here and Now: Lasting Happiness You Can Count On

Happiness is a skill that can be learned, not something you're born with.

Happy Here and Now teaches you that skill, in straightforward language with real-life examples.

Then it shows you how to make happiness a habit in your life.

What brings real happiness is the knowledge that it's lasting and not a fleeting experience that shows up when something wonderful happens.

Happy Here and Now offers the tools that will make happiness dependable in your life.

Happy Here and Now will show you how to have the life you want, filled with good relationships, meaning, and a deep feeling of contentment that isn't dependent on what may come.

Want to be happier? Read *Happy Here and Now*

www.ingramcontent.com/pod-product-compliance
Lightning Source LLC
Chambersburg PA
CBHW060944050726
47592CB00003B/1097